PASSOVER UNLEAVENED BREAD

CHELSEA KONG

Ceremonial Children's Guide

© 2019-2021 Chelsea Kong

All rights reserved. All images used in this book are licensed copies from their respectful owners including myself and Freepik, Pixabay, Canva, and Pexels. This book or any portion thereof may not be reproduced or used in any manner whatsoever even with the written permission of the publisher. All content in this book is only permitted to be used for teaching and not for sale.

Printed in 2019-2021
IBSN: 978-1-990399-18-3
Library and Archives Canada

Passover

Jesus is the Passover Lamb.

He took away our sins and all people's sins.

Passover is one of the Bible feasts.

What is Passover?

It is a celebration to remind us of when God delivered Israel out of Egypt from slavery.

God also killed the firstborn of Egypt and asked the Jews to put the blood of the Lamb on the doorposts to keep them safe.

They are to celebrate this for 7 days to eat the bread without yeast and eat for all 7 days.

Why do we celebrate it?

Jesus also celebrated Passover before He was taken to die on the cross.

It reminds us of the slavery in Egypt that Israel suffered and how God brought them out of it.

We celebrate it to remind us of what God did in saving us from sin.

Passover tells us about Jesus Christ who paid for our sins and died on the cross for us.

He is the lamb that has no spot
and nothing wrong with Him.

He never sinned against God, but
He took our place as a perfect lamb.

How to prepare for Passover

God's people had to clean their house and make sure there is no yeast.

God told the children of God to prepare a lamb with no spots and nothing wrong with it.

Take unleavened bread, which is bread made without yeast, which the Jews call matzah.

We also need to clean our hearts from any sin we have done.

The Passover Meal

The plate must have bitter herbs like lettuce and parsley, horseradish, a lamb bone, an egg, and the matzah should be separated with three pieces piled like a sandwich. The middle piece has a paper towel or cloth wrapping it.

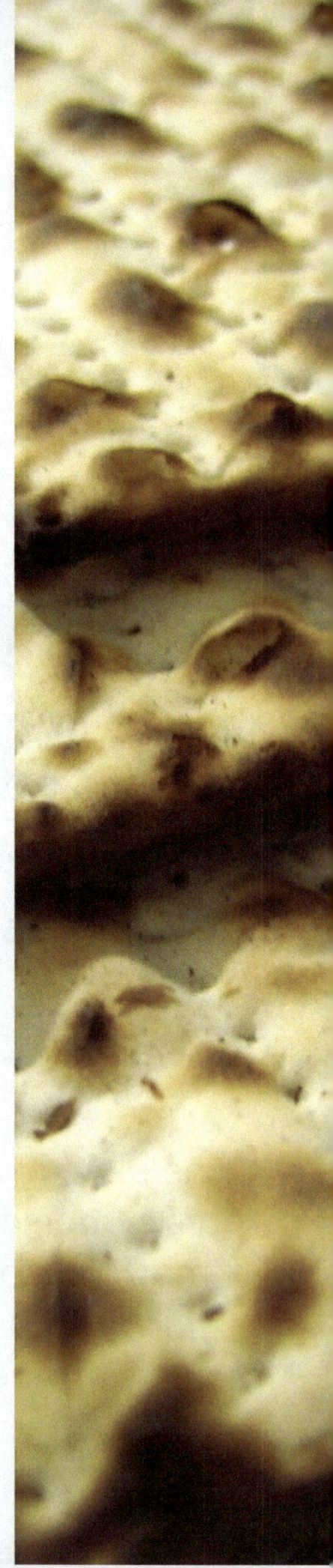

It means Father, Son, and Holy Spirit because Jesus died and was put in the tomb and then be was raised and now lives forever.

There should be 2 candles and some matches, 4 cups of grape juice or wine, a bowl of saltwater, charoseth (a paste of nuts, apples, pears, and wine).

Who should celebrate it?

People that believe in God can celebrate it and friends.

This will open the door for them to be saved when they eat the meal and take the Holy Communion.

Your family can do this at home and it can be for the full 7 days of the celebration.

Your father and mother and children should be at the table

Jesus and His disciples sat with their
left arm on the table and leaning forward,
which means we are free people.

Jesus also said that He is the bread from heaven.

The Ceremony

Kadesh – the Benediction in Hebrew and English.

The mother has to say a blessing over the candles and then light the candles.

Blessed are You, O Lord, our God, King of the universe, who has set us apart by His word, and in whose name we light the festival lights.

Four Cups

God says, "I will" (Exodus 6:6-7)

1. Cup of Sanctification means to be holy.
God made the separation between
the Jews and the Egyptians.

Pour a small amount of juice or wine into the cup
and wait. One cup can be used for all 4 cups.

2. Cup of Judgement is to make a good decision.

God judged Egypt.

3. Cup of Redemption means saved from evil.

God saved us from our sins through Jesus Christ.

4. Cup of Praise means to be accepted.

We will be with Jesus and also drink this cup with Him in heaven.

1st Kiddush: Cup of Santification

Everyone is asked to raise the first cup.

Then the blessing is said over the cup.

Blessed are You, O Lord, our God, King of the universe, Creator of the fruit of the vine.

We can now take the first cup of grape juice or wine.

Wash your hands

You can wash your hands if you want as part of the meal.

It means to be clean from sin.

You don't have to do this, but the Jews did this before they eat the meal.

Blessing the Karpas

The father at the table is to take the karpas or lettuce to dip into the bowl of saltwater and it is a bitter herb.

He is to give one to everyone at the table, doing the same thing.

Then everyone must say this blessing over it before eating it

Blessed are You, O Lord, our God, King of the universe, Creator of the fruit of the earth.

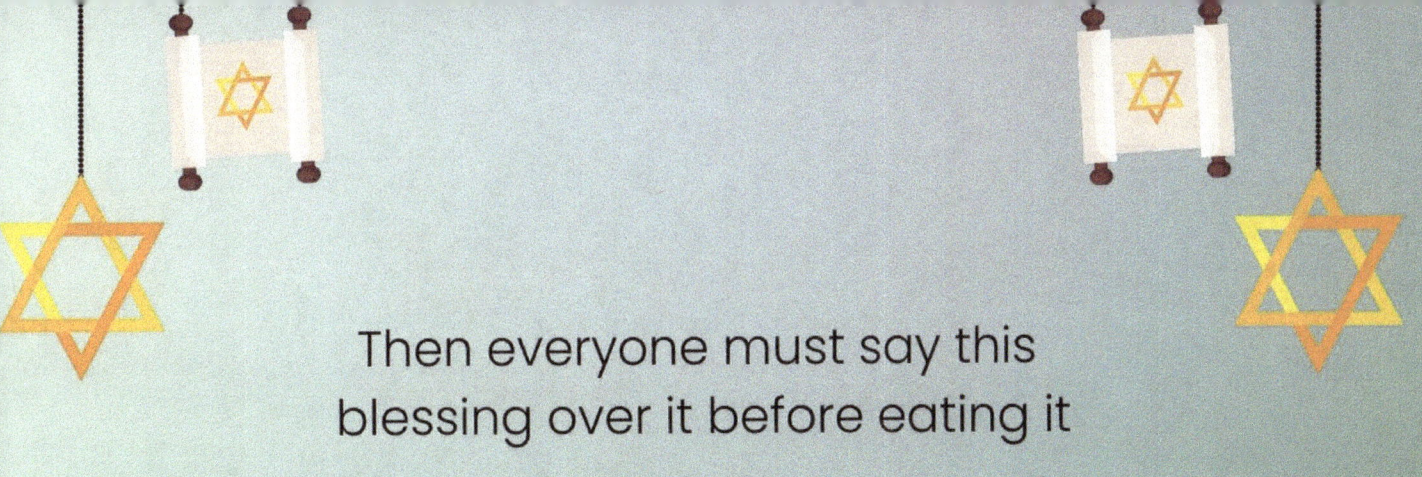

Why you must eat the Karpas

It is to remind God's people of the bitterness they had in Egypt because they did slave labour to make bricks for Pharoah.

They had hard lives in Egypt because they had to work hard.

Pharoah hated and was afraid of Israel and wanted to stop them from growing in number.

Afikomen – Unleavened Bread in half

Afikomen means the one that comes after, which is the middle piece of bread.

Jesus Christ is the Unleavened Bread that died and was put into the tomb and then he was raised from the dead to be in heaven.

The bread must be broken into two pieces
because Jesus was broken for us.

One half is to be hidden away. The children have to
find it by the end of the meal before the third cup.

It will be used for Holy Communion
and the second cup is poured.

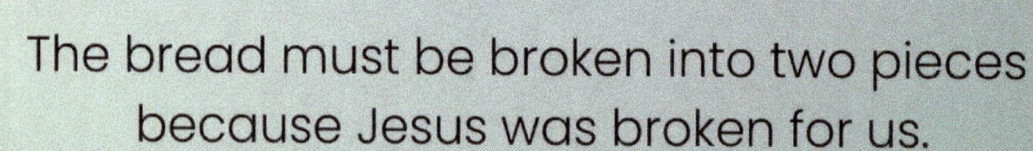

In the next step, the child or children will read the Passover story and then ask four questions.

God's people had to work hard slave labour in Egypt. God told Moses that he will kill the firstborn sons of Egypt. He sent Moses to tell the people to get a lamb and to take its blood and to put the blood on the top and sides of the door frame so that when the angel of death comes, it will pass over those in the home. They will be safe. He also told the people to prepare a lamb enough for one family and they must eat it and leave nothing behind. The rest they must burn with fire. They must make the bread without yeast and they must eat this quickly because they must leave Egypt quickly.

Maggid: Passover Story

The Four Questions

Why is this night different from all other nights?

1. On all other nights, we eat either leavened or unleavened bread; why on this night do we eat only matzah which is unleavened bread?

2. On all other nights, we eat vegetables and herbs of all kinds; why on this night do we eat only bitter herbs?

3. On all other nights, we never think of dipping herbs in water or in anything else; why on this night we dip the parsley in salt water and the bitter herbs in charoseth?

4. On all other nights we eat either sitting upright or reclining, why on this night do we all recline?

The Four Answers

Why is this night different than other nights?

1. Jews go from slavery to freedom.

We eat unleavened bread because there is no time to bake bread, there is no time to wait for the yeast to rise! We must leave quickly!

2. We eat bitter herbs because our forefathers were slaves in Egypt and their lives were made very bitter!

The Four Answers

3. We dip the herbs twice because it is the green of springtime and our forefathers withstood bitter slavery as the hope of freedom sweetened it!

4. Tonight we all recline at the table because reclining was a sign of a free man long ago, and our forefathers were freed on this night!

God's Plan

Child reads

But I know that the king of Egypt will not let you go unless a mighty hand forces him. So I will raise my hand and strike the Egyptians, performing all kinds of miracles among them. Then at last he will let you go. (Exodus 3:19-20)

On that night, I will pass through the land of Egypt and strike down every first-born son and firstborn male animal in the land of Egypt. I will execute judgment against all the gods of Egypt, for I am the Lord!

Passover in the Torah

The Jews read about Passover from the Torah.

This is the original writing of the Bible.

In those days, scribes would write on sheets that were sown together and made into scrolls.

Today, scrolls are made of regular paper and this is the Old Testament part of the Bible.

2nd Cup: The Cup of Judgement

God sent 10 plagues against Egypt to judge the people and the land.

Blood, frog, gnats, flies, pestilence, boils, hail, locusts, darkness, and the death of firstborn.

This is when we drink the second cup and then the dinner can be eaten.

It is when the bitter herbs are blessed and then we can eat.

Blessed are You, O Lord our God, King of the universe, who made us holy in His commandments, and commands us about the eating of bitter herbs the charoseth.

Blessing of the bitter herbs

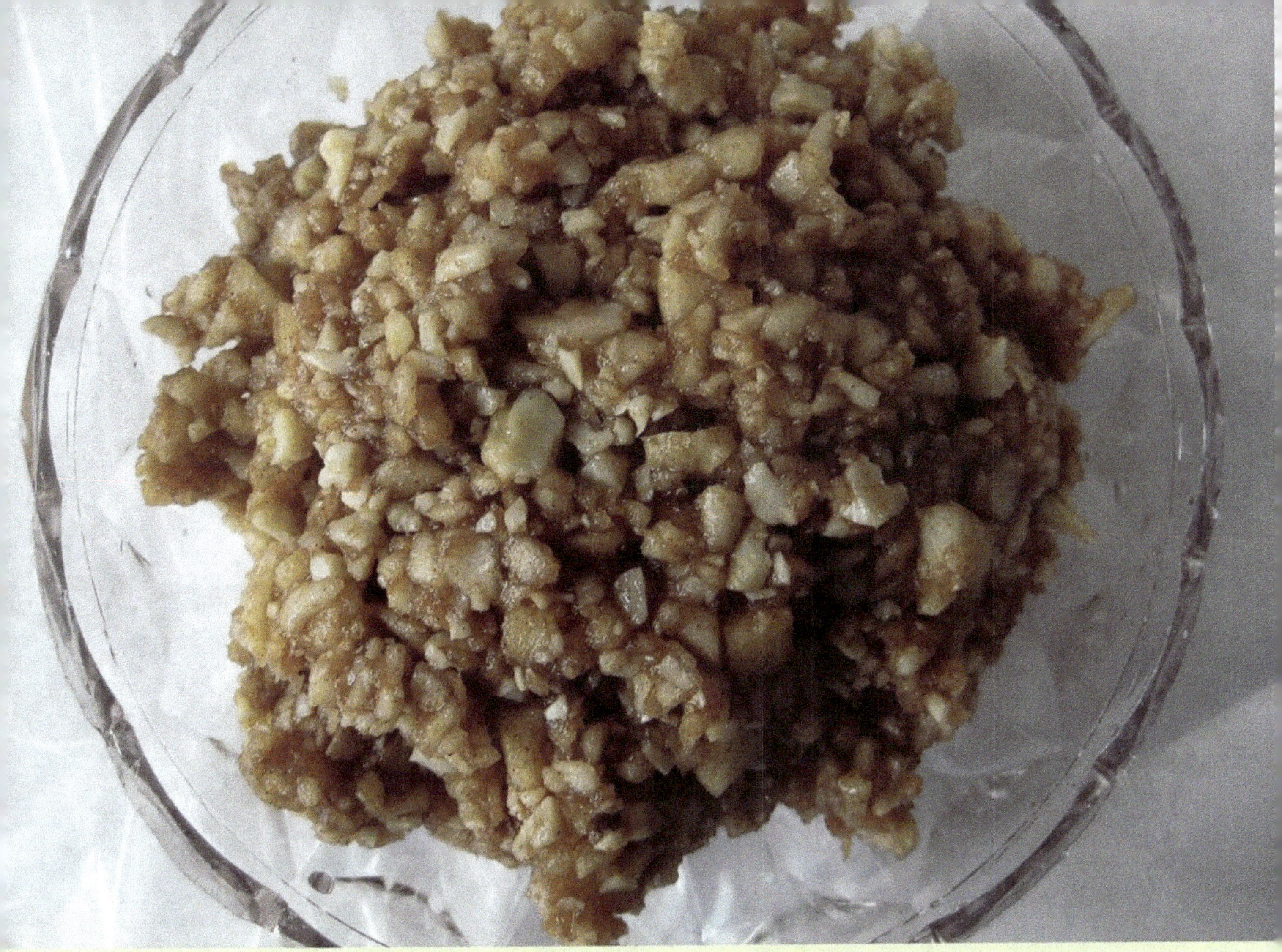

Take the one half of the middle to share and you can eat it with some charoseth and the parsley. You eat it like a small sandwich.

This is the bitter and the sweet, which means God's people remember the goodness of God in the time of the bitter life they had.

Charoseth

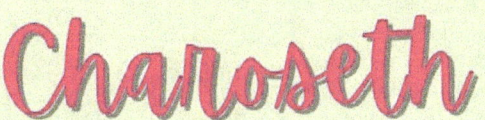

There is an egg for each person, so there were no animals to sacrifice because the temple was destroyed.

The lamb bone on the seder plate means there is no need for any more sacrifices because Jesus is the perfect sacrifice.

He is the Lamb that was paid the price for our sins.

Egg and Lamb Bone

Pray and bless the food before you eat it.

They eat the lamb and have chicken soup or fish soup to go with the meal.

They have an egg with the meal.

They are to eat all the food that is on the table and make room for the Holy Communion after the meal is done.

The Dinner Meal

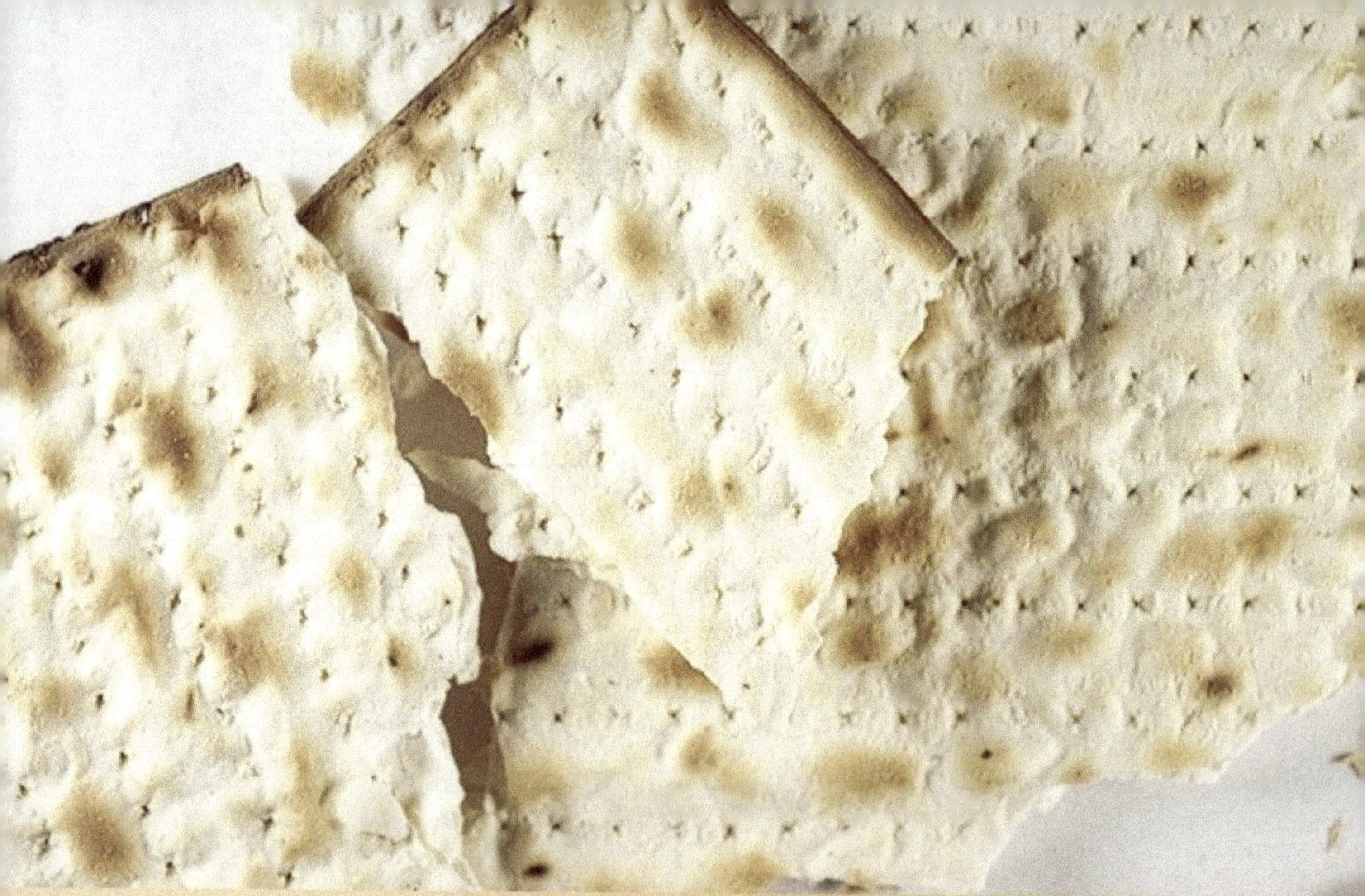

The children must find the Afikomen.

It is to be broken into pieces for
Holy Communion to give to each person

It means that Jesus Christ was buried
in the tomb and rose from the dead.

We have a new life in Him, and when we take this, it
is like eating His body.

Afikomen

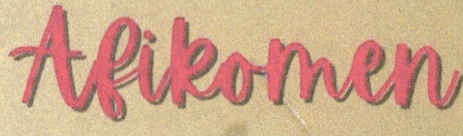

3rd Cup: The Cup of Redemption

The third cup is poured out.

The third blessing is said before we drink the cup.

Blessed are You, O Lord, our God, King of the universe, Creator of the fruit of the vine.

The cup is His blood that was poured out for us to cover our sins.

The next is to do the Holy Communion.

Holy Communion Means

Holy Communion is Jesus Christ's body broken for us.

When we believe in Him, He will have His eternal life.

The bread is His body and also for giving us health, healing, and all the blessings.

But he was pierced for our transgressions, he was crushed for our iniquities; the punishment that brought us peace was on him, and by his wounds we are healed. (Isaiah 53:5)

Holy Communion in the Bible

For I have received of the Lord that which also I delivered unto you, that the Lord Jesus the same night in which he was betrayed took bread:

And when he had given thanks, he brake it, and said, Take, eat: this is my body, which is broken for you: this do in remembrance of me.

After the same manner also he took the cup, when he had supped, saying, this cup is the new testament in my blood: this do ye, as oft as ye drink it, in remembrance of me. (1 Corinthians 11:23-25)

We can say the Hebrew blessing when the Holy Communion is done.

It's time to confess and repent to God for the sins that we did against Him, others, and ourselves.

Confess, Repent, and Forgive

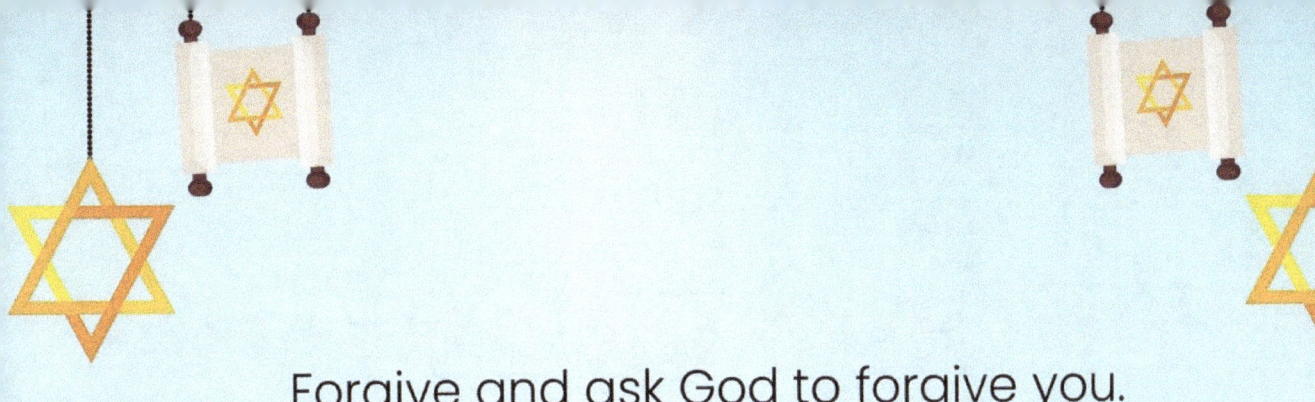

Forgive and ask God to forgive you.

Then we can take the bread and the cup to remember Jesus and what He did.

We can get healed, restored, and blessed.

Welcomes the prophet

 There should be a place at the table that is empty with a plate, fork, knife, spoon, napkin, and cup for Elijah.

You need to make sure that there is an empty spot and a full table set for him.

It is to expect his return.

If the door is already open, it must be closed.

Somebody is asked to go to the door to open it and see if Elijah is coming and when we don't see, that person must come back to the table.

4th Cup: Cup of Salvation and Blessing

Pour out the fourth cup.

This cup is a prophetic act, which means are drinking the cup in faith believing that we are with Jesus in heaven.

He will drink this cup with us at the wedding feast for those who are His.

The blessing is spoken over the last cup before you drink it

Blessed are You, O Lord our God, King of the universe, Creator of the fruit of the vine.

To close we say "See you next time in Jerusalem."

SALVATION PRAYER

God, I know I sinned against you. Forgive me for the wrong that I have done. I believe that Jesus Christ died on the cross for me. That He rose from the grave so that after three days. I can have His long-lasting life. Come into my heart to be my Lord and Savior. I choose to turn away from my sins and I choose to follow you. Lead me to walk with you. Keep me safe and teach me your ways. Stop every bad thing in my life that has an open door to hurt me. Close those doors. Holy Spirit, fill me now in Jesus' name. Amen.

BAPTISM IN THE HOLY SPIRIT 🔥

Jesus, you are the one that fills me with Your Spirit. Come, Holy Spirit, and come into my life and fill me to overflow with Your presence. Come with your fire too. Thank you for the gift of tongues in Jesus' name. Amen.

Open your mouth and let the words come out that God gives you. It will be words you don't know what they mean. You can ask God what it means. You need to let Him talk through you every day to grow this gift.

PRAYER

Father God, make us ready for your return. That we will stay close to you. Put it in my heart to love others. Help me share with them about you. Lead my steps every day. Keep me in your way. I want to be in your Kingdom forever. Save those who I love in Jesus' name. Amen.

Message from the Author

We need to be ready for Jesus' return. Stay in God's love and keep in Him. Stay away from the wrong people. Obey Him and go where He leads you. He will keep you if you decide to stay with Him. Pray for those you love. Pray for those God shows you and tells you to pray for. Share with them about Jesus. Jesus is coming back for His Bride. Those who belong to Him will do what He says and live forever. They will live with Him in His Kingdom. They will never die.

OTHER PRODUCTS

- Knowing God
- How to Hear God's Voice
- New Life in Jesus
- Loving Israel
- God's Gifts/Spiritual Talents
- Meeting God
- Word Power
- Fruit of the Spirit
- The Tabernacle
- Bride for Jesus
- A Life of Prayer
- Live Free
- Who am I in Jesus
- Walk in Love
- God's Favor
- Man of God
- Woman of God
- How to Use Money
- God's Wisdom
- Fasting
- See Jerusalem and Bethany
- First Fruit Offering
- Feast of Trumpets
- Day of Atonement
- Feast of Tabernacles
- Counting the Omer
- Festival of Lights
- Glory, Presence, and Holy Spirit
- Live in God's Presence
- Pentecost
- 31 Day Devotional
- Biblical Puzzle Book Vol 1
- Biblical Puzzle Book Vol 2
- Biblical Puzzle Book Vol 3
- Biblical Puzzle Book Vol 4
- Biblical Puzzle Book Vol 5
- Bible Puzzles for Young Children Book 1
- Bible Puzzles for Young Children Book 2
- Bible Puzzles for Young Children Book 3
- Biblical Puzzle for Children Books 1-3
- How God Speaks
- Knowing Jesus
- Knowing Holy Spirit
- A Healthy Life and A Healthy Life Work Book
- Smokey the Cat

OTHER PRODUCTS

Teaching Series
How to Hear God's Voice Teaching Guide & Audio Book
Relationship with God, Jesus, Holy Spirit Guide
Knowing God, Jesus, Holy Spirit Guide & Audio Book
Flowing in the Prophetic

Teaching (Non-Sale on my website)
Purim
Passover
Resurrection

More books to come!

More books on Amazon, Kobo, and Barnes and Noble
https://chelseak532002550.wordpress.com/

Review

More books on Amazon, Kobo, and Barnes and Noble
https://www.amazon.com/author/chelseakong

Please leave a review and share with friends to help the author continue to write more books to reach more readers. Thank you so much for your support.

About
CHELSEA KONG

She is a writer, creative arts and digital media artist, skilled administration professional, and podcaster. Chelsea also served in a variety of roles, from audiovisual, photography, to assisting on the worship team, and ministry team. She also has a passion for families being united.

Chelsea has been a guest on Unity Live Radio and The Lady Tracey Show and is highly recommended by a Proud Christian blog. She graduated from Hotel and Restaurant Management, Digital Media Arts, Office Administration, and experience working with children. Chelsea lives in Toronto, Canada. She mainly writes children's books, stories, bridal writing, poems, lyrics for songs, words of encouragement, blessings, prayers, and jokes. The author of How to Hear the Voice of God, the Bridal Collection, Knowing God, etc. She also has her own Bible Puzzle books and other inspired products. Her podcast channel is called Chelsea K on Anchor, Spotify, and iTunes.

Please check my website to find out more:
https://chelseak532002550.wordpress.com/

www.ingramcontent.com/pod-product-compliance
Lightning Source LLC
Chambersburg PA
CBHW060410010526
44107CB00005B/641